D0504530

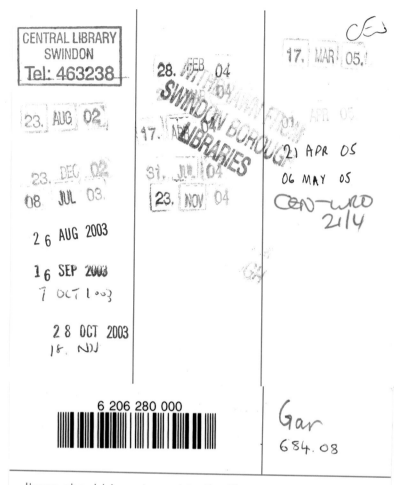
Items should be returned to the library from which they were borrowed by closing time on or before the date stamped above, unless a renewal has been granted.

Swindon BOROUGH COUNCIL

SBC.LIB 02

GREEN WOOD
FOR THE GARDEN

GREEN WOOD
FOR THE GARDEN

15 easy weekend projects using freshly cut wood

Alan and Gill Bridgewater

NEW HOLLAND

First published in 2002 by New Holland Publishers (UK) Ltd
London • Cape Town • Sydney • Auckland

Garfield House, 86–88 Edgware Road, London W2 2EA, United Kingdom
www.newhollandpublishers.com

80 McKenzie Street, Cape Town, 8001, South Africa

Level 1, Unit 4, 14 Aquatic Drive, Frenchs Forest, NSW 2086, Australia

218 Lake Road, Northcote, Auckland, New Zealand

ISBN 1 85974 989 5 (hardback)

Editorial Direction: Rosemary Wilkinson
Project Editor: Clare Johnson
Production: Hazel Kirkman

Designed and created for New Holland by AG&G BOOKS
Designer: Glyn Bridgewater
Illustrator: Gill Bridgewater
Project design and woodwork: Alan and Gill Bridgewater
Photography: AG&G Books
Editor: Fiona Corbridge

Reproduction by Modern Age Repro House Ltd, Hong Kong
Printed and bound in Malaysia by Times Offset (M) Sdn. Bhd.

CONVERSION CHART

To convert the metric measurements given in this book to imperial measurements, simply multiply the figure given in the text by the relevant number shown in the table below. Bear in mind that conversions will not necessarily work out exactly, and you will need to round the figure up or down slightly.

(Do not use a combination of metric and imperial measurements – for accuracy, keep to one system.)

To convert	*Multiply by*
millimetres to inches	0.0394
metres to feet	3.28
metres to yards	1.093
sq millimetres to sq inches	0.00155
sq metres to sq feet	10.76
sq metres to sq yards	1.195
cu metres to cu feet	35.31
cu metres to cu yards	1.308
grams to pounds	0.0022
kilograms to pounds	2.2046
litres to gallons	0.22

CONTENTS

INTRODUCTION

When we were first married, we used to enjoy going on day-long rambling walks in the woodlands around our country cottage home. Our memories are of hot days with dappled sunlight shimmering through the trees, and the continual quest for the perfect place for a picnic. One such walk led us deeper and deeper into a great forest, and we became worried about losing our way. Then we pushed through the trees into a sunlit glade, and there in front of us stood a woodcutter's cottage complete with a sawing horse, a log pile and a mountain of wood shavings.

Making green wood furniture and other structures for the garden is a creative and therapeutic activity, which anyone can enjoy.

The whole cottage looked as if had been fashioned out of the forest. The gate was made from rough, riven boards, the door latch was a gnarled crutch, the bridge over the brook consisted of a couple of fallen trees, the porch posts were tree sections; even the shed was built in the style of a log cabin. Items made from green wood were everywhere – bird houses, hay rakes, brooms, clothes pegs, porch chairs – all beautifully made from fresh-sawn logs that had been variously riven, left in the bark, bent, and shaped with saw, axe and knife. For us, it was a vision of how life could be, and we were entranced.

From then on, we had a dream to aspire to. We would buy a small woodland lot and build a log cabin cottage. We would have a couple of children, grow our own food, swap our car for a horse, and build our furniture from green wood. Of course, we now know that our dreams were the enthusiasm of young love, but despite that, from that day to this, we have always tried in a modest way to hold true to our romantic vision. Alongside our other homebuilding activities – including working with stone, designing water gardens and woodcarving – we have, wherever possible, used green wood for building structures.

Working with green wood has various advantages. The basic raw materials are readily available and relatively cheap, and the techniques required are straightforward and easily learnt. You don't need a workshop filled with expensive machinery and a wide range of tools. For the projects in this book, you only need a few uncomplicated tools. If you have a garden with a patch of lawn, and a lean-to shelter to store your wood and tools, the rest is simple. Making garden furniture and structures doesn't get any easier than this.

Not so long ago, the practice of working with green wood had fallen out of favour, but it is now an inherent part of the fast-growing popular movement to conserve our native forests. If you like the idea of collecting green wood, splitting it with an axe, cutting basic joints, and then using the items that you have made to embellish your home and garden, you will find this book stimulating and rewarding.

Best of luck.

Alan & Gill

HEALTH AND SAFETY

Many woodworking procedures are potentially dangerous, so before starting work on the projects, read through the following checklist:

- ☞ Make sure that you are fit and strong enough for the task ahead. If you have any doubts about your health, ask your doctor for advice.

- ☞ When using an axe, ensure that you are working at a comfortable height, with your legs well braced, and with your hands and legs away from the arc of swing. Check that nobody else is nearby.

- ☞ Whenever possible, use battery-powered tools rather than those with cables.

- ☞ Always use a safety electricity circuit breaker between the power socket and your mains power tools, to protect you from electric shock.

- ☞ If components or completed sections are heavy, ask friends to help you lift them.

- ☞ Keep a first-aid kit and telephone within easy reach, in case of emergencies.

- ☞ If your children want to be involved, let them watch at a safe distance, or help with small tasks, but never leave them unsupervised.

ABOUT GREEN WOOD

*I*t's a wonderfully uplifting experience to cut down a section of coppice (or even to buy the wood ready felled) and then to convert the posts, poles, rods and wands into items for the porch and garden. The smell of the sap and the feel of the tools will transport you to the world of a cottage woodsman or that of an American pioneer.

THE HISTORY OF GREEN WOOD

Green wood is freshly cut wood that is still in its wet or "green" state, as opposed to dried, seasoned wood. Traditionally, a woodsman used wood not long after it had been cut, whereas a carpenter worked with prepared sections. Working with tools such as a saw, axe and drawknife, woodsmen converted trees and coppice into everything from gates and fence hurdles to rakes, scythe handles, clogs, chairs, brooms, hoops and tent pegs.

Unfortunately, since the timber trade was mechanized in the 1940s (allowing whole trees to be mechanically dried, sliced up and run out as standard sections), green wood activity has, to a great extent, fallen into decline. However, the good news is that there is currently a revival of interest in green wood products, with a new generation of craftspeople making everything from porch chairs to benches, garden shelters, gates, bird houses, screens, hurdles, trugs and orchard ladders.

MATERIALS

Green wood, the basic raw material, can be obtained as large-section timber in the form of rough-sawn boards or riven posts and rails, and as small-section coppice wood in the form of poles, rods and wands. Large-section timber is obtained by felling whole trees and sawing the trunk into planks and boards, while small-section coppice wood is produced by cutting certain trees back to ground level, and then using the cluster of straight growth that springs up from the tree bole.

The definitions of words used to describe coppice, such as post and pole, vary according to region, so the best thing to do is to go to the supplier armed with a list of sizes. An added complication is the fact that coppice wood is, by its very nature, thicker at one end than at the other. For the projects in this book, our definitions are as follows. Wands range in diameter from 5 mm to 15 mm, rods from 15 mm to 40 mm, poles from 40 mm to 80 mm, and posts from 80 mm to 150 mm.

All green wood, from large sections to small sections, should be purchased from managed woodlands that are carefully cropped and tended, rather than woodlands that are stripped and then left. Using green wood in this way shows a respect for nature – it's the right and proper way to use wood to its best potential in your area. Other materials such as nails, wire and twine can be sourced from general DIY stores.

A coppice woodland. The growth from the bole of trees that have been coppiced (cut back to ground level) is used for small-section green wood such as poles, rods and wands, ranging from 5 mm to 80 mm in diameter.

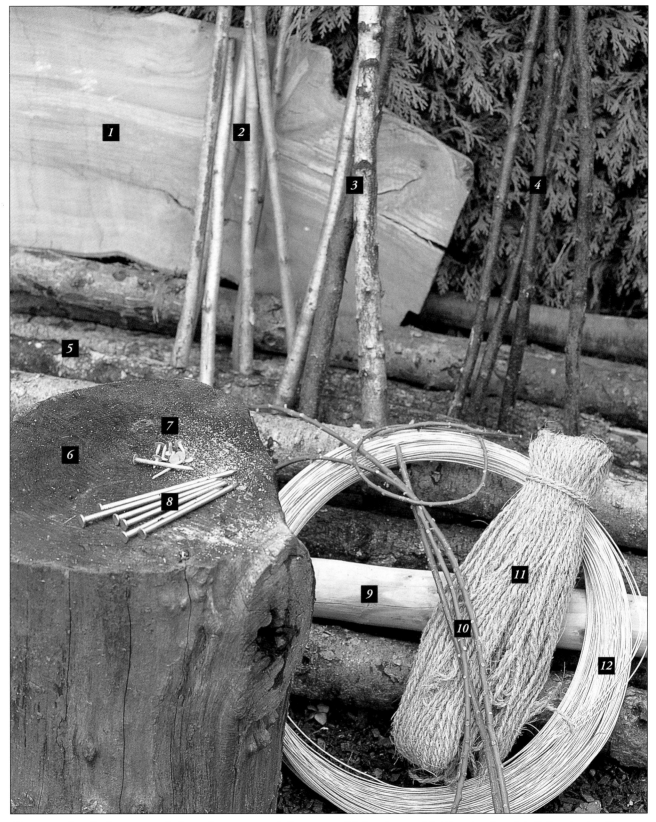

Green wood and other materials for making projects (other species of wood may be used). *(1)* Sawn green plank. *(2)* Hazel rods. *(3)* Mixed poles. *(4)* Beech coppice rods. *(5)* Larch post. *(6)* Chopping log. *(7)* Galvanized nails. *(8)* Steel nails. *(9)* De-barked larch post. *(10)* Holly wands. *(11)* Natural twine. *(12)* Galvanized wire.

TOOLS

Working with green wood isn't an exact science. Because of its random nature *(loose bark, tapering sections, knots, and all manner of bends and twists),* a lot of the measuring, marking and cutting can be done by eye. So study the unique shapes of your wood, measure and cut generously oversize, and then trim back to best fit. All the tools featured here are available from general DIY stores.

TOOLS FOR MEASURING AND MARKING

Tape measure

Pencil

Reel tape measure

Spirit level

You need two types of rule for measuring: a large, flexible reel tape measure for setting out site plans and for measuring lengths and girths, and a flexible metal measure for all the general sizing. If you can afford the extra cost, choose a fibreglass reel tape measure, because they are hard-wearing, don't buckle or snap, and it doesn't matter if they get wet. You will also need a good-size spirit level and a supply of carpenter's flat-lead pencils. Buy the cheapest spirit level available and then you won't be too upset if it gets crushed.

TOOLS FOR CUTTING WOOD

Secateurs

Loppers

Jigsaw

Crosscut saw

You need a general-purpose, coarse-toothed crosscut saw for cutting boards, posts, poles and thick rods; a pair of long-handled loppers or secateurs for cutting thin rods and thick wands, hand secateurs or pruners for cutting thin wands, and a power jigsaw for cutting curves in boards. Because green wood is generally wet, gritty, bark-covered, knotty, and sticky with sap and resin, we recommend that you purchase top-quality loppers and hand secateurs (because they can be cleaned and sharpened easily) and cheap, throwaway saws.

TOOLS FOR MAKING JOINTS

Chisel

Axe

Mallet

Wire cutters

Cordless drill

Club hammer

Claw hammer

Long-nosed pliers

You need eight basic tools for making joints in green wood. We use a small axe for rough shaping and stripping off bark, a mallet and chisel for making precise cuts, a cordless drill for drilling pilot holes prior to nailing, a claw hammer for banging in nails, a club hammer for use as an anvil when clenching over the points of nails, wire cutters and pliers. If you decide to use a mains power drill, make sure that you use it in conjunction with a safety electricity circuit breaker. Choose a good-quality axe – we use a hand-forged black iron axe, made in China. It didn't cost much; nevertheless it is a top-quality tool. It is just the right weight, the blade is thin and double-bevelled, and the handle is well shaped, made from straight-grained wood and comfortable to hold. If you need to cut costs, it may be possible to purchase secondhand tools from a car boot sale or fleamarket.

OTHER USEFUL TOOLS

You need a pair of portable workbenches for most sawing and jointing tasks, a chopping log when using the axe, and a stepladder for high-reach projects such as the "Tea for Two" Shelter. For one or two of the projects you will also require a garden spade for levelling sites and digging holes for posts, a standard sledgehammer for banging in posts, and a piece of 20 mm-thick, exterior-grade plywood for use as a ground-level workboard.

GREEN WOOD TECHNIQUES

W*orking with green wood in the garden is an enjoyable activity to undertake. Anyone who can hold a saw, trim bark with an axe and bang in a nail, is capable of making all the projects. If you are ready to let the natural shape of the wood be your guide, you will find that the techniques are as easy as... falling off a log.*

MEASURING AND MARKING

Much of the measuring is best done by eye. Hold the wood in place, mark the line with the saw and then make the cut.

Marking out
Use a tape measure, pegs and string to establish the size and position of the structure

Squareness
To ensure that the shape has 90° corners, the diagonals must be an identical length

When working with unevenly shaped wood, a spirit level can only give an overall estimation of the accuracy of horizontal positioning.

Peg out a rectangle, with opposite sides of equal length. Measure the distance between the diagonals at each end, add the measurements together and divide by two. Adjust the pegs so that both diagonals conform to this measurement.

These procedures of measuring and marking are carried out with a tape measure, spirit level, and your eyes. We usually measure and cut the component parts so that they are oversize, and then make final adjustments by eye. When working with green wood and testing with the measure and spirit level, you have to go for the best overall fit and squareness. (A good way of testing the accuracy of a square or a rectangle is to make adjustments until the diagonal measurements are identical.)

When using green wood, you have to work with round sections that are, to various extents, tapered, bent and twisted. You have to be flexible in your approach, and remember that the whole essence and character of green wood forms is that they are less than perfect.

SAWING, LOPPING AND AXING

Use a general-purpose, coarse-toothed saw for making straight cuts in slabs of wood and for cutting large-diameter, round-section wood (greater than 20 mm in diameter).

Curved shapes
A jigsaw's narrow blade allows you to guide the saw along curved lines

When you need to cut out curved shapes from slabs of wood, use an electric jigsaw. Fit a blade with teeth of a size that relates to the thickness of the material you are cutting. A jigsaw is not suitable for cutting round-section wood.

Normally, we advocate using quality traditional tools for most jobs; however, sawing green wood is one of the few tasks that is best achieved with a cheap, general-purpose, coarse-toothed saw. The reason is that the wet, sappy, resinous wood is so hard on the teeth that a saw only lasts for a couple of projects. Whether using a hand saw or a jigsaw, we usually do the sawing close to where the project will be sited, with the workpiece either leaning against, or clamped in, the portable workbench.

When it comes to cutting rods and wands, you have to decide whether to use long-handled loppers or hand secateurs. Although much depends upon the hardness of the wood being worked, we usually choose loppers for thick wood and hand secateurs for thin wands. When using the loppers, you will find it much easier to cut at a low angle, so that you make a long, low, shearing cut angled to the run of the grain.

When using an axe, you need a chopping block to work on. A tree stump measuring approximately 400 mm in diameter and 600 mm high is ideal. When making a glancing cut – as you might do when pointing a post or shaving off an area of bark – nail a strip of wood across the chopping block to act as a stop. This will prevent the piece of work sliding away from the axe. It is better to use several light, well-aimed blows to shape the wood you are working on, rather than attempting to axe the shape in one go, which frequently results in taking off more than you intended.

Use a pair of loppers for cutting small-section wood to length (wands and rods between 10–20 mm in diameter).

Axing
Take several shavings to achieve the shape you want

Chopping block
You will need a block to support the workpiece

A sharp axe is ideal for carving wood to shape. Use it to create pointed or flattened ends on rods and poles.

CUTTING JOINTS

To make an angled half-lap joint, clamp the post in a vice and start by sawing halfway through its thickness.

Using an axe like a chisel, hit it with a piece of wood to split out the waste from the half-lap joint.

To level a section of a component in preparation for jointing, use a broad chisel to shave away the wood.

Jointing green wood involves taking two or more component parts – posts, poles, rods or wands – and fixing them together so that they become a strong and stable whole. However, the thing that makes green wood jointing so challenging is the fact that the components are randomly round in cross-section and tapered in length. In general terms, there are two ways of creating a joint. You can butt the two parts together bark to bark, in which case there is very little contact between the components and the joint ends up being relatively weak. Alternatively, you can use a combination of saw, axe and chisel to cut part of the rounded surfaces of the components to a level finish before butting them together. The levelling option results in a stronger joint.

BENDING AND WEAVING

Bending
The wood must be bent around the curve gently so that it does not break

Wands of wood can be carefully bent around a curve provided that the wood has been harvested recently.

Alternating thicknesses
Weave the wood so that a thin end lies alongside a thick end

Beating back
As you weave, push each piece tightly against the previous piece

Weaving wood in and out of a frame (or posts stuck in the ground) creates an attractive screen, border or fence.

Projects such as the Country Club Chair (see page 66), Warp and Weft Woven Border (see page 30), and Hearts and Diamonds Screen (see page 58), require wood that can be bent. Depending on the project, it may be better to use a thin wand that can be bent easily into a tight circle, as in the Classical Cone project (see page 34), or wood that can be bent into a broad curve, as for the chair and the screen. While many types of wood can be bent, we favour using holly for tight curves, and young hazel and beech for broad curves. Wood harvested in the spring bends more easily than wood cut in winter. Always use local wood from a renewable resource.

DRILLING AND NAILING

Before nailing (especially near the end of a piece of wood) drill a hole through the top piece of wood.

If the work bounces around when you are trying to nail, use a club hammer to help support the wood.

For added strength, use a nail that is long enough to go through both components, then bend the end over.

Once the wood has been cut and jointed, the joint has to be nailed. Depending upon the situation, the nail might run through one component and part-way into another, or right through both components.

Always drill pilot holes prior to nailing, to minimize the risk of splitting the wood. Use a drill bit that is slightly smaller than the diameter of your chosen nail. If a joint's strength and stability are crucial to the project, you can go one step further. First, drill right through both components. Using an extra-long nail, hammer it all the way through both pieces of wood so that the point sticks out of the other side. Finally, clench the end of the nail down against the workpiece, or if possible, bend it over so that the point re-enters the wood.

BINDING

Natural twine
Use string or twine made from natural materials

Wired joint
Use three loops of wire for each joint

Flexible wood
Green holly is woven into a hoop or "quoit"

A binding of green wood can be added to a twine binding, to strengthen the joint and improve its appearance.

Wired joints are employed when the wood is too thin to nail successfully. Loops of wire are tightened with pliers.

We use thin, galvanized wire for binding jointed bent wood, where there is a lot of stress on the joints created by springing one length of wood against another; string or twine for binding bundles, as in the Obelisk project (see page 42); and thin holly wands for binding items such as the wreaths used in the Classical Cone project (see page 34). When gathering holly, go for the new green growth, rather than last year's wood, as it's both easy to cut and supple. Always seek the owner's permission before helping yourself to wood.

THE
PROJECTS

*In the lists of materials, the
measurements given for length refer
to the wood as you would buy or
harvest it. The measurements
specified for the diameter of sticks
should be treated as a guide.*

BEEHIVE CLOCHE

Reminiscent of the glass bell or cloche that was popular with gardeners in Victorian and Edwardian times, this beautifully decorative woven beehive cloche will both protect and shape young plants. Place the beehive over tender shoots or flowers to provide a barrier that is attractive to look at and perfect for keeping pets and children at bay.

YOU WILL NEED

Materials for a beehive cloche approximately 600 mm high and 1 m in diameter.

☙ Beech coppice: 8 rods, 3 m long and 15 mm in diameter (arches, hoops and diagonal ties)

☙ Logs: 4 short logs about 100 mm in diameter

☙ Galvanized wire: small roll of soft 1 mm wire

☙ Steel nails: 9 x 150 mm

☙ Ball of thin cotton twine or cord

☙ Ball of coarse natural fibre twine (as used to tie up plants)

Tools

☙ Pencil and flexible rule

☙ Pliers

☙ Wire snips

☙ Long-handled loppers or secateurs

☙ Hand secateurs or pruners

PERSPECTIVE VIEW OF THE BEEHIVE CLOCHE

Bound joint
The arches are tied together with natural twine

Arch
15 mm rod cut to fit

Small hoop
15 mm rod bent to make a hoop 530 mm in diameter

Diagonal tie
15 mm rod cut to fit

Large hoop
15 mm rod bent to make a hoop 960 mm in diameter

Wired joint
3 loops of twisted wire hold the hoop together

HOW TO MAKE THE BEEHIVE CLOCHE

1 Gently ease and bend the straightest, most flexible beech rod to make a hoop 960 mm in diameter. Bind the overlapping ends of the rod together with three wire ties. Check that the structure is secure and trim the ends of the rod. Repeat this procedure to make a second hoop 530 mm in diameter.

2 Set the large hoop on the grass, resting it on the four short logs. Spike nails in the grass at the centre of the hoop and around the edge, just like the points of a compass. Link the nails with ties of thin cotton twine so that the circle is divided into eight wedges. The twine marks the position of the arches.

3 Trim a beech rod to a length of 2 m, and bend it into an arch. Spike the ends of the arch into the grass on the inside of the hoop, so that it bridges the diameter of the circle. Continue pushing the ends of the rod into the grass until the peak of the arch stands about 500 mm high from the grass.

4 Make three other arches as described in Step 3, in order to create the characteristic beehive shape. Use wire to lash the arches securely to the hoop. Ease the ends of the arched rods out of the grass and remove the logs, twine and nails. Trim the ends of the arches so that the beehive stands 600 mm high.

5 Bind the topmost intersection of the arches with coarse twine so that you finish up with a large, ball-like knot that holds the structure together securely. Drop the second hoop over the beehive, level it by eye, and lash it in place with wire.

6 Trim offcuts of beech rod to fit diagonally across the eight "windows" framed between the two hoops and the curves of the arches. Fix them in place with wire. Finally, tidy up all the ends of the wood and wire with secateurs and wire snips.

DESIGN VARIATIONS

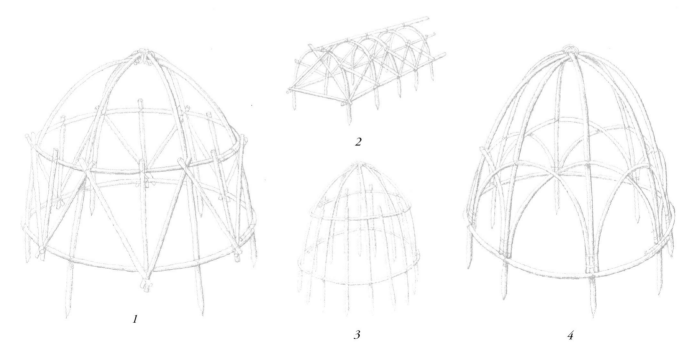

2

1

3

4

(1) A simple cloche with straight, zigzag bracing struts.
(2) A seed-bed tunnel made from a number of hoops and straight bracing struts. *(3)* A cloche with closely spaced, pet-proof bars. *(4)* A cloche with bent hoop bracing.

ARCHED TREFOIL TRELLIS

*T*his delicate trellis was inspired by the spidery rustic woodwork that was favoured in the late nineteenth century, especially in cottage gardens. The diamond lattice and the trefoil tracery infill at the top of the Roman arch combine to make a beautifully subtle garden feature, which is perfect for twining with roses, or using as a backdrop to add vertical interest to a flower border.

YOU WILL NEED

Materials *for a trellis approximately 2.34 m high and 850 mm wide.*

- Beech coppice: 4 poles, 2 m long and 25 mm in diameter (main frame)

- Beech coppice: 6 rods, 2 m long and 20 mm in diameter (lattice ties)

- Beech: 3 wands, 2 m long and 15 mm in diameter (arch)

- Holly: 3 wands, 1 m long and 10 mm in diameter (trefoil decoration)

- Galvanized nails: 1 kg pack of 75 mm x 3.75 mm

- Galvanized wire: small roll of soft 1 mm wire

Tools

- Pencil and flexible rule

- Long-handled loppers or secateurs

- Plywood workboard

- Cordless drill

- Drill bits to match the size of your nails

- Claw hammer

- Club hammer

- Pliers

- Wire snips

- Hand secateurs or pruners

FRONT VIEW
OF THE TRELLIS

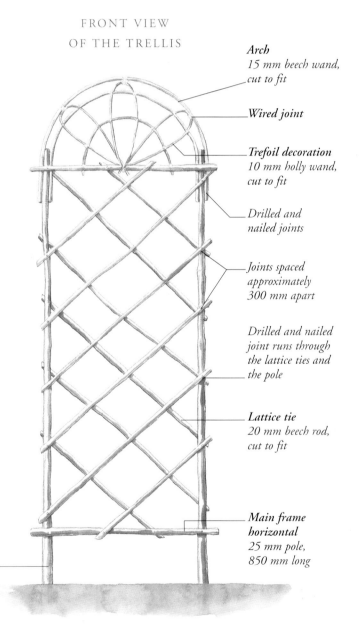

Arch
15 mm beech wand, cut to fit

Wired joint

Trefoil decoration
10 mm holly wand, cut to fit

Drilled and nailed joints

Joints spaced approximately 300 mm apart

Drilled and nailed joint runs through the lattice ties and the pole

Lattice tie
20 mm beech rod, cut to fit

Main frame horizontal
25 mm pole, 850 mm long

Main frame vertical
25 mm beech pole, 2 m long

HOW TO MAKE THE ARCHED TREFOIL TRELLIS

1 Cut the three beech poles for the main frame to length with the loppers, making two at 2 m (for the verticals) and two at 850 mm (for the horizontals). Set the verticals flat on the workboard, so that they are parallel and 674 mm apart. Drill and nail the two horizontals in place – one 300 mm up from the bottom and the other about 100 mm down from the top. Turn the frame over and use the claw hammer to bend the points of the nails over.

2 Mark off the vertical poles at intervals of 300 mm, and mark centre-points on the two horizontals as a guide to fixing the lattice. Position the 20 mm-diameter beech rods for the six diagonal lattice ties on one side of the main frame. Use the loppers to trim the rods to length. Drill and nail the intersections.

3 When you have fixed the lattice ties on one side of the main frame, turn the frame over and repeat the procedure on the other side, using the remaining six diagonal lattice ties to form the diamond pattern of the lattice. Use the two hammers to clench the points of the nails: place the nail head on the head of the club hammer (using it like an anvil) and with the claw hammer, bend the point of the nail around and down so that it re-enters the wood.

4 Take two of the 15 mm-diameter beech wands and bend them repeatedly until they are supple and flexible. One piece at a time, drill and nail one end at the top of one side of the frame. Bend the wand over to make a pleasing symmetrical arch and then drill and nail the other end to the other side.

5 Bend the three holly wands until they are flexible. Loop them so that the ends cross, and bind the intersections with wire. Fit the three loops within the arch and wire them in place. Finally, use the last beech wand to make the lower inner arch, wiring it in place. Neaten ends with the secateurs.

DESIGN VARIATIONS

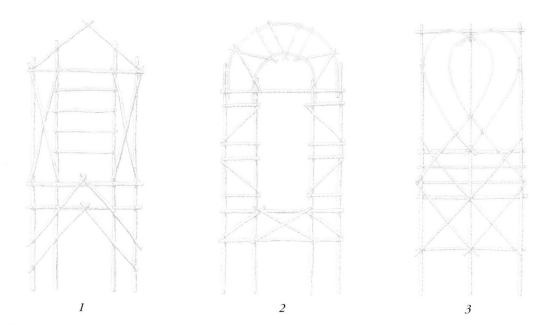

1   *2*   *3*

(1) A pediment trellis (with a simple triangular top) can be made entirely from straight components. (2) This Classical-style trellis has an arched top (as in this project) with a column at either side. (3) A trellis reminiscent of American folk art. This is more complex and uses heart and diamond motifs to both decorate and brace the structure.

BIRD HOUSE FEEDER

This visually exciting garden feature will attract lots of birds to the garden, with the added advantage that the birds will help you rid the garden of all manner of insect pests. Our design echoes an original Victorian feeder that we once saw in a gamekeeper's cottage garden. It is beautiful in its massive simplicity, made from rough-sawn slab wood throughout. The whole structure is held together with nails.

YOU WILL NEED

Materials for a bird house feeder approximately 560 mm high and 700 mm wide.

- Hardwood (rough-sawn, with waney edges kept intact): 1 x 3 m length, 500 mm wide and 20 mm thick (floor, under-floor, walls, roof, wall fixing strips)

- Beech coppice: 2 poles, 2 m long and 30–40 mm in diameter (ridge pole, roof finials and cladding for the side walls)

- Larch feature post: about 2 m long and 100 mm in diameter, with a fork at the top end (mounting post)

- Galvanized nails: 1 kg pack of 75 mm x 2.65 mm

- Galvanized cap-end roofing nails: 2 x 75 mm

- Steel screws: 4 x 50 mm no. 8

Tools

- Pencil, flexible rule, square and spirit level
- Portable workbench
- Electric jigsaw
- Cordless drill
- Twist bits to fit the various nail sizes
- Claw hammer
- General-purpose, coarse-toothed saw
- Small axe
- Chopping log
- Screwdriver
- Spade

PERSPECTIVE VIEW OF THE BIRD HOUSE FEEDER

Roof finial
30–40 mm beech pole, 150 mm long

Ridge pole
30–40 mm beech pole, 480 mm long

Roof
20 mm hardwood, 480 mm long and 310 mm wide

Doorway
260 mm high and 200 mm wide

Cladding
30–40 mm beech pole, 310 mm long

Side wall
20 mm hardwood, 239 mm high and 310 mm wide

Front gable wall
20 mm hardwood, 360 mm square

Wall fixing strip
20 mm hardwood, 310 mm long and 20 mm square

Floor
20 mm hardwood, 700 mm wide and 400 mm deep (the 20 mm hardwood under-floor piece, hidden from view, is 300 mm square)

Mounting post
100 mm larch post, 2 m long, with forked branches at the top

HOW TO MAKE THE BIRD HOUSE FEEDER

1 Set out the floor, under-floor, side walls, front and back gable walls, roof slabs (wancy edges left intact), and the strips for fixing the walls to the floor. Cut out the parts with the jigsaw.

2 Drill and nail the gable walls directly to the side walls. The positioning doesn't need to be too exact, as long as the four walls are square to each other, so that the house sits square and firm.

3 Nail the two wall fixing strips in place on the floor slab, so they are 240 mm apart on the outside edges. (Drill pilot holes through the strips first, in order to avoid splitting the wood.)

4 Position the two roof slabs directly on top of the gable walls, so that the underside faces of the slabs meet along the line of the ridge, and the edges are well aligned. Drill and nail them in place, with the nails centred in the thickness of the wall.

5 Cut the remaining poles into 310 mm lengths, then with the axe, split them carefully along their length. Drill and nail these half-log sections on the side walls. Make the finials by trimming two waste pieces of beech coppice with the axe.

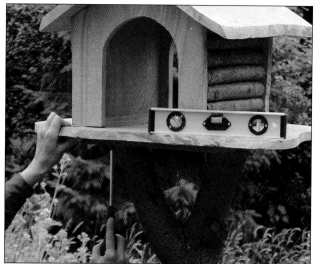

6 Cut the ridge pole for the roof to length, and then drill and nail it in place with the two cap-end roofing nails, inserting the nails so that they run down into the top edges of the front and back gable walls. Drill and nail the finials to the ends of the ridge pole.

7 Drill and nail the under-floor slab directly to the top of the forked mounting post, and then sit the house on the slab and run screws up from the underside. Dig a hole and erect the mounting post, siting it away from structures that could give cats easy access.

DESIGN VARIATIONS

1

2

3

(1) *This simple four-stick design is very easy to clean.*
(2) *Design based on a tribal hut in New Guinea.*

(3) *A two-storey design incorporating arches, with a straight mounting post and added bracketing pieces for support.*

WARP AND WEFT WOVEN BORDER

S*hop-bought woven hurdles and garden screens undoubtedly have their merits, but making your own woven in-bark wood items produces a much more natural effect than factory-sawn laths and slats. It is also possible to build structures to fit the unique shape of your garden. All you do is bang in the warp poles, so that about half their length is in the ground, and then weave the weft rods in and out to make the infill.*

YOU WILL NEED

***Materials** for a woven border approximately 300 mm high and 5 m long.*

☞ Mature beech coppice: 3 poles, 2 m long and 40–50 mm in diameter (vertical posts – warp)

☞ Beech coppice: 16 rods, 2 m long and 10–15 mm in diameter (woven infill – weft)

☞ Galvanized nails: 1 kg pack of 75 mm x 3.75 mm

Tools

☞ Pencil and flexible rule

☞ Portable workbench

☞ General-purpose, coarse-toothed saw

☞ Chopping log

☞ Small axe

☞ Sledgehammer

☞ Claw hammer

☞ Long-handled loppers or secateurs

☞ Club hammer

PERSPECTIVE VIEW OF THE WOVEN BORDER

Vertical posts are spaced 400 mm apart

***Vertical post** 40–50 mm pole, 500 mm long*

***Woven infill** 10–15 mm rods, in 2 m lengths*

Topmost rods are nailed to the vertical posts with 75 mm nails

Vertical posts are sharpened to a point and go 200 mm into the ground

HOW TO MAKE THE WOVEN BORDER

1 Saw the three 2 metre-long beech poles into quarters to make vertical posts about 500 mm long. Next, shape one end of each post to a point. Set the chopping log at a comfortable working height. Nail a piece of scrap wood to the log to act as a stop. Butt a post up against the stop, and use the axe to sharpen its end to a point. Repeat for the other posts.

2 Cut a 400 mm-long measuring stick from a piece of waste wood to use as a spacer to mark the distance between the vertical posts along the length of the woven border. Take the sledgehammer and bang the vertical posts into the ground to a depth of about 200 mm, so that they stand proud by 300 mm. Be careful not to split the posts.

3 Taking one beech rod at a time, weave it in and out of the vertical posts to form the woven infill. The characteristic pattern is achieved by alternating the rods so that the thick end of one rod is set against the thin end of another.

4 When you come to join rods, use the loppers to trim the end of the old rod close to the post it has just cleared. If possible, join the new rods so that the thick ends overlap the thin. They do not need to be nailed.

5 As you work, beat the rods down so that they fit together in both plan and front view. Spend time choosing the rods you use, so that the various dips and bends of the wood mesh together for a close fit and pleasing appearance.

6 Finally, when you have woven as many rods as possible into the 300 mm height of the vertical posts, use the claw hammer, as shown, to nail the topmost rods to the vertical posts. Use the club hammer to support the post whilst nailing.

DESIGN VARIATIONS

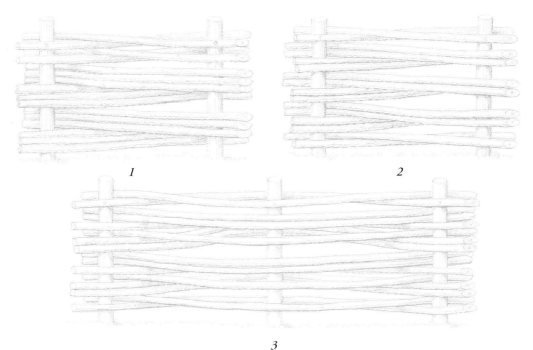

1

2

3

(1) A simple design with four sticks woven normally at the top, and the other sticks woven in groups of three.

(2) Another design using groups of two sticks. (3) A more complicated design with the appearance of a random pattern.

CLASSICAL CONE

O*f all the geometric motifs traditionally used in gardens, such as obelisks, cubes and spheres, the cone has long been the most popular, from carved stone cones on plinths to yew trees sculpted into dramatic, giant freestanding cones. If you would like a green wood cone to grace your garden – as a frame for a climbing plant, or simply as a design statement – this one can be made quickly and easily.*

YOU WILL NEED

Materials *for a cone approximately 2 m high and 600 mm in diameter.*

- ❧ Holly: 12 wands, 2 m long and 10 mm in diameter (quoits)

- ❧ Beech coppice: 16 poles, 2 m long and 25 mm in diameter (verticals)

- ❧ Galvanized wire: small roll of soft 1 mm wire

- ❧ Ball of coarse natural fibre twine (as used to tie up plants)

Tools

- ❧ Pencil and flexible rule

- ❧ Long-nosed pliers

- ❧ Scissors

- ❧ Long-handled loppers

- ❧ Hand secateurs

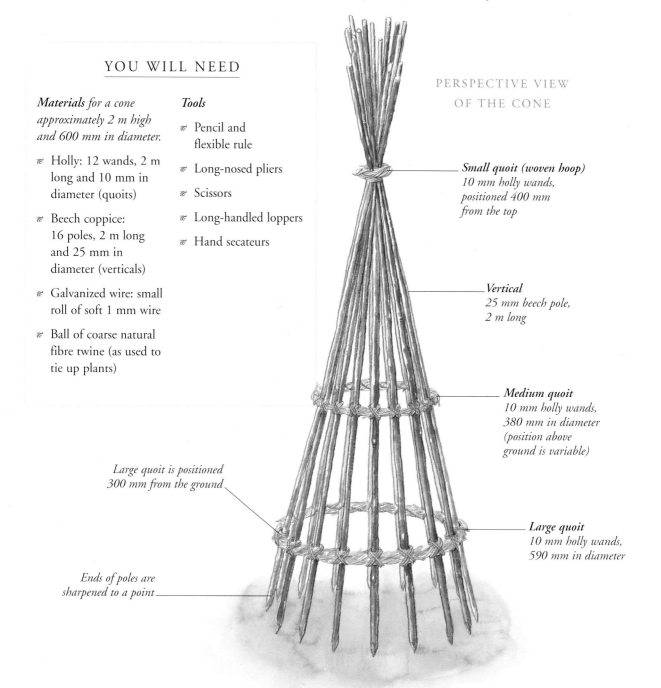

PERSPECTIVE VIEW
OF THE CONE

Small quoit (woven hoop)
10 mm holly wands, positioned 400 mm from the top

Vertical
25 mm beech pole, 2 m long

Medium quoit
10 mm holly wands, 380 mm in diameter (position above ground is variable)

Large quoit is positioned 300 mm from the ground

Large quoit
10 mm holly wands, 590 mm in diameter

Ends of poles are sharpened to a point

HOW TO MAKE THE CLASSICAL CONE

1 First, make the large quoit or woven hoop. Gently flex the strongest holly wand over your knee to create a rough hoop measuring about 590 mm in diameter, and allowing a good overlap at the two ends. Wrap three bindings of wire over the overlap, one at each end and one in the middle, tightening them with the pliers.

2 Take some of the softer, more flexible lengths of holly and wind them in and around the basic hoop until you have a large, fat quoit resembling a Christmas wreath. Wire the ends as necessary. Repeat the procedure to make the medium quoit measuring 380 mm in diameter.

3 Set the large quoit on the grass and spike the sixteen 2 m beech poles into the ground around it, positioning them at the eight compass points, and at the eight points between these.

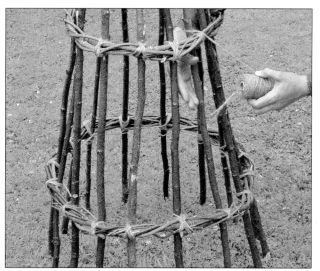

4 Lift the quoit upright, then pull it out through the beech poles. Gather the poles at a point about 400 mm from the top, and bind them with twine. Take the remaining lengths of holly wand and wind them in and around the bound area to cover the twine and make the small quoit.

5 Drop the large quoit over the cone and ease it into a position about 300 mm above the ground. Wind and tie twine over each of the sixteen intersections of the poles and quoit. Repeat the procedure with the medium quoit. Use the loppers and secateurs to trim all the ends of the poles and wands.

DESIGN VARIATIONS

1

2

3

(1) An attractive, natural-looking design incorporating untrimmed twigs at the tops of the poles.

(2) An onion-shaped design with four bent poles. (3) A helter-skelter design braced with a spiral of woven wands.

RUSTIC SLABWOOD GATE

This is a copy of a cottage gate that we made when we were doing our best to live self-sufficiently. The original was made from rough-sawn, waney-edged slab wood obtained free from the local sawmill, plus poles donated from a neighbour's copse, all held together with nails. The hinges and the latch were also made from wood.

YOU WILL NEED

***Materials** for a gate approximately 1.2 m high and 680 mm wide.*

☞ Mature beech coppice: 4 posts, 2 m long and 80 mm in diameter (fenceposts)

☞ Beech coppice: 10 poles, 3 m long and 40–50 mm in diameter (gate hinge rails, fence rails and poles, gate stops)

☞ Rough-sawn hardwood: 3 waney-edged slabs, 2 m long, 200–250 mm wide and 20–25 mm thick (gate uprights and gate ledges)

☞ Beech coppice: 2 crutches, about 300 mm long and 30–40 mm in diameter (gate latch and catch)

☞ Galvanized nails: 1 kg pack of 40 mm x 2.65 mm

☞ Steel nails: 1 kg pack of 100 mm x 4.5 mm, and 1 kg pack of 125 mm x 5.6 mm

☞ Steel washers: 5 washers to fit the 125 mm-long nails

☞ Two buckets of hardcore (broken brick or rubble)

Tools

☞ Pencil and flexible rule

☞ Portable workbench

☞ General-purpose, coarse-toothed saw and jigsaw

☞ Small axe

☞ Chopping log

☞ Cordless drill

☞ Twist drill bits to fit the various nail sizes

☞ Claw hammer

☞ Large bevel-edged chisel

☞ Mallet

☞ Spade

☞ Sledgehammer

PERSPECTIVE VIEW OF THE GATE

Gate stop 40–50 mm beech pole, 1.3 m long. Nailed to fencepost so it's flush with the ground

Small gate upright 20–25 mm hardwood, 200–250 mm wide and 1.15 m long

Gate catch and latch Beech crutches

Gate ledge 20–25 mm hardwood, 200–250 mm wide and 680 mm long

Large gate upright 1.2 m long

Fencepost 80 mm beech post, 1.3 m long

Gate hinge rail 40–50 mm beech pole, 750 mm long (extends beyond gate upright by 100 mm)

"Clear swing" notch 55 mm wide, 69 mm deep

Fence pole 40–50 mm beech pole, 1.2 m long

Fence rail 40–50 mm beech pole, 2 m long

HOW TO MAKE THE RUSTIC SLABWOOD GATE

1 Cut the three slabs for the gate uprights. Cut the tops of the slabs to a rough point with the jigsaw. Position the slabs side by side, spacing them to make a total width of 700 mm.

4 Measure and mark two "clear swing" notches on the hinge side of the gate, just below the top hinge rail and just above the bottom hinge rail (as shown on the working drawing). These stop the fence rails hindering the opening of the gate. Use the saw, chisel and mallet to remove the waste.

2 Cut each of the three gate ledges to length (680 mm). Use the axe to skim the sawn ends to a rough chamfered finish, with the chamfer on the same side as the waney edge.

3 Fix the ledges with 40 mm nails (two on one side of the gate to support the hinge rails, and one on the other side). Nail the hinge rails on the other side of the ledges with 40 mm nails.

5 Cut the 80 mm-diameter beech fenceposts to length. Set the gate in position, with temporary poles to hold it upright and to distance it from the ground. Dig holes for the posts, stand them in place, and use the sledge-hammer to ram hardcore around the posts.

6 Fix the fence rails to the fenceposts, extending them by 100 mm on the hinge side. Fix the poles to the rails, placing them 50 mm above the ground and 50 mm apart. Use 100 mm nails.

7 Rest the top hinge rail on the extended fence rail and drill a 5.6 mm hole through both. Put a washer between them and a nail (125 mm) to act as a hinge pin. Repeat for the other hinge.

8 Fashion the catch and latch. Nail the catch to the gatepost, and fix the latch to the gate ledge with a nail and washers. Nail the gate stops to the fenceposts. Use 100 mm nails throughout.

DESIGN VARIATIONS

1

2

3

(1) A classic design with symmetrical arched top. (2) An American folk art design with heart motif and crossed braces. (3) A traditional English country cottage gate with pointed pickets and crossed braces.

OBELISK

I*f you enjoy growing annual climbing plants in the flower or vegetable garden, you will be able to put this project to good use. It will display sweet pea flowers to best advantage, or enable you to grow your runner beans without the need for battalions of sticks. The wigwam is an attractive structure that will enhance your garden, unlike eyesores made from ecologically unfriendly plastic mesh.*

YOU WILL NEED

Materials *for an obelisk approximately 2.5 m high and 830 mm square.*

- ✎ Hazel coppice: 12 poles, 3 m long and 25 mm in diameter (vertical poles)

- ✎ Beech coppice: 12 rods, 3 m long and 15 mm in diameter (horizontal ties)

- ✎ Galvanized wire: small roll of soft 1 mm wire

Tools

- ✎ Pencil and flexible rule

- ✎ Hand secateurs or pruners

- ✎ Pliers

- ✎ Wire snips

PERSPECTIVE VIEW OF THE OBELISK

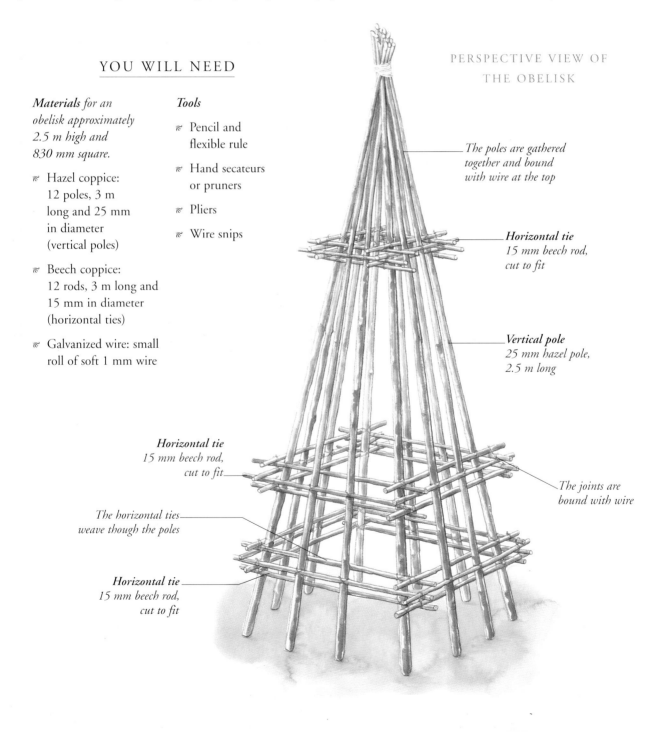

The poles are gathered together and bound with wire at the top

Horizontal tie 15 mm beech rod, cut to fit

Vertical pole 25 mm hazel pole, 2.5 m long

The joints are bound with wire

Horizontal tie 15 mm beech rod, cut to fit

The horizontal ties weave though the poles

Horizontal tie 15 mm beech rod, cut to fit

HOW TO MAKE THE OBELISK

1 Cut and trim the twelve hazel vertical poles to a length of 2.5 m. Using offcuts to map out the arrangement on the grass, lay two poles on the grass to make an inverted "V" shape, with the heel ends placed about 830 mm apart. To form the horizontal ties, lay beech rods across the "V" at points 300 mm, 600 mm and 1.5 m up from the heel end, and trim them to fit. Bind the intersections with wire.

2 Make another identical frame, then stand them both upright so that the four heels mark out an 830 mm square, and the horizontal tie rods are on the outside of the frame. Cut additional horizontal ties to link the other sides of the two frames, wiring them firmly in place.

3 Stand two more vertical poles against each side of the frame, placing them on the outer side of the horizontal ties. Neighbouring poles should be about 276 mm apart at the heels. Wire the vertical poles to the horizontal ties at each intersection, binding them firmly.

4 Weave and wire two more horizontal ties alongside each of those already in place, so that each horizontal bar is made up from three rods. Tighten the wire bindings with pliers until the sticks are pulled close together and the joints are secure.

5 When you are pleased with the wigwam's overall shape, gather the twelve vertical poles at the top and lash them together with wire to hold them firm. Finally, use the secateurs to trim the ends of all the poles and rods to a tidy finish.

DESIGN VARIATIONS

1

2

3

(1) A traditional design with crossed bracing rods at the sides.
(2) A design with four single diagonal braces at the base, and
horizontal rods. (3) A long-braced design, which creates a
strong structure suitable for very windy gardens.

LOG CABIN PLANTER

*W*ith its strong, direct lines, this big, bold planter looks like an American log cabin in miniature. The side panels consist of horizontal cladding poles nailed to corner posts. If you enjoy working with large-section wood, and you would like to build a sturdy container suitable for a large shrub or a small tree, this project is ideal.

YOU WILL NEED

Materials for a planter approximately 780 mm high and 700 mm square.

- Larch poles with the bark removed: 24 poles, 2 m long and 60 mm in diameter (for cladding the side panels and floor)

- Larch poles with the bark removed: 2 poles, 2 m long and 77 mm in diameter (corner poles)

- Beech coppice: 4 rods, 2 m long and 20 mm in diameter (decorative motif)

- Galvanized nails: 0.5 kg pack of 40 mm x 2.65 mm nails

- Steel nails: 2 kg pack of 125 mm x 5.6 mm nails

Tools

- Pencil, felt-tip pen and flexible rule

- Crosscut saw

- Plywood workboard about 1.5 m square

- Masking tape

- Electric drill with drill bits to fit your nail sizes

- Very strong cord or thin rope: about 4 m

- Claw hammer

- Long-handled loppers or secateurs

PERSPECTIVE VIEW OF THE PLANTER

Decorative motif
20 mm beech rods

*Fixed with 40 mm
galvanized nails*

*First pole is fixed
100 mm from the bottom
of the corner poles*

Corner pole
77 mm larch pole,
780 mm long

Side panel cladding
60 mm larch pole,
640 mm long

*Fixed with
125 mm steel nails*

HOW TO MAKE THE LOG CABIN PLANTER

1 Cut 36 identical pieces of cladding, 640 mm long, from the 60 mm-diameter larch poles. On the plywood workboard, make a simple jig to fit one of the pieces. Place a masking tape marker 38 mm from one end of the jig, and another 98 mm from the other end of the jig. Fit the drill with a bit to match the 125 mm nails, and bore two holes in each cladding pole.

2 Cut the four corner poles. Measure 100 mm up from the foot end of each pole and mark (position of the base). Cut a piece of offcut wood to a length of 427 mm, to make a spacer, and use cord to lash it from the top of one corner pole to another. Nail the pre-drilled cladding poles between the two corner poles with 125 mm nails. This forms one side panel.

3 Make another side panel, as described in Step 2. Lash both panels together with the cord and offcut as a spacer, as already described, and nail all the other cladding poles in place with 125 mm nails, completing the other two side panels and forming an open-ended box. Be careful that the spacer doesn't fly free whilst you are nailing.

4 Cut the remaining 60 mm-diameter larch poles into lengths of 581 mm, for the eleven poles that make the planter's base. Turn the box on its side, so that you are looking into the bottom end. Nail two of the poles to bridge the corner poles, making bearers to support the base. Angle the nails in order to give the base maximum strength.

5 Stand the box on its feet and then drill and nail the other nine poles across the bearers with 125 mm nails. (Two of the poles must be cut to 427 mm to fit between the corner poles.)

6 Stand the box on its feet and saw the tops of the four corner poles across at an angle to make a decorative face that slopes outwards. Trim all pole ends to a tidy fit with the loppers.

7 Tip the planter on its side, with the best side uppermost. Using the loppers, cut the beech rods to length for your chosen decorative motif, then fix in place with 40 mm nails.

DESIGN VARIATIONS

1

2

3   *4*

(1) *A planter with a trellis for climbing plants (the back posts extend upwards to form a frame for the trellis).* **(2)** *A low planter for holding small plants.* **(3)** *A planter with a straightforward vertical stripe motif.* **(4)** *A classic planter with a traditional diamond motif.*

AMERICAN BACKWOODS BENCH

There is nothing quite so pleasant as relaxing on a bench that you have made yourself. Drawing inspiration from early American backwoods furniture, this bench is easy to make, comfortable to sit on, and good to look at.

YOU WILL NEED

Materials for a three-seater bench, about 2 m long.

- Beech mature coppice: 10 poles, 2 m long and 40–50 mm in diameter (legs, long rails and diagonal rail to link the ends of the bench, short stretchers to link the legs, diagonal end braces, armrest supports)

- Beech mature coppice: 1 bow-shaped pole, 2 m long and 50–60 mm in diameter (top rail that forms the curved backrest)

- Beech mature coppice: 2 well-matched poles, 1 m long, which curve and taper from 60 mm in diameter down to 50 mm (components for the two armrests)

- Hazel or beech bends and crutches: a selection (decorative apron)

- Hazel coppice: 30 straight rods, 2 m long and 25–30 mm in diameter (seat, back and trim rail)

- Steel nails: 1 kg pack of 150 mm x 6 mm

- Galvanized cap-end roofing nails: 1 kg pack of 75 mm

- Galvanized nails: 1 kg pack of 125 mm x 5.6 mm, 1 kg pack of 100 mm x 4 mm

Tools

- Pencil and flexible rule

- Portable workbench

- General-purpose, coarse-toothed saw

- Small axe

- Chopping log

- Cordless drill

- Twist bits to fit the various nail sizes

- Claw hammer

- Club hammer

- Long-handled loppers or secateurs

PERSPECTIVE VIEW OF THE BENCH

Back leg
40–50 mm beech pole,
840 mm long

Short stretcher
40–50 mm beech pole,
540 mm long

Front leg
40–50 mm beech pole,
560 mm long

Trim rail
25–30 mm hazel rod,
cut to fit

Long rail
40–50 mm beech pole,
1.7 m long

Back
25–30 mm hazel rod,
750 mm long

Top rail
50–60 mm beech pole,
2 m long

Armrest
60–50 mm beech pole,
650 mm long

Armrest support
40–50 mm beech pole,
590 mm long.
(Offcut between
supports – spacer)

Seat
25–30 mm hazel rod,
500 mm long

Diagonal end brace
40–50 mm beech pole,
cut to fit

Diagonal long rail
40–50 mm beech pole,
cut to fit

HOW TO MAKE THE AMERICAN BACKWOODS BENCH

1 Saw the beech poles for the front and back legs to size. Cut the four short stretchers to length, and use the axe to skim the ends to a flat-faced finish. Set the components together, with the stretchers roughly 200 mm apart. Drill pilot holes, and fix the joints with clenched 150 mm nails.

2 Set the two bench ends back to back, square them up by eye and cut, drill and nail two diagonal end braces with 100 mm nails, in order to brace and hold the bench ends square. The nails are clenched over tightly on what will be the inside face of the legs.

3 Bridge the bench ends with the four long rails (note flat faces). Drill holes through the rails and legs; fix the joints with clenched nails. Fix the top rail. Use 150 mm nails throughout.

4 Fit the armrest support, using 150 mm nails. Skim a flush top face on the spacer. Run 150 mm nails through the supports, capturing the spacer. Nail the armrests with 100 mm nails.

5 With the loppers, cut 26 rods, 500 mm long, for the seat. The back requires 21 rods, 750 mm long. Use the axe and the chopping log to skim the ends to a flat-faced finish, as shown.

6 Make the seat. Drill and nail the two end rods to the frame with 100 mm nails. Drill and fix the trim rail to the ends of the two rods using cap-end roofing nails. Using one of the seat rods as a spacer, nail the other seat rods to the frame with cap-end roofing nails – so that they are square and the front ends butt on to the trim rail. Place the seat rods so that the best face is uppermost. Trim off any sharp knots.

7 Make the back. Set two back rods in place either side of the central rod and fix them with roofing nails. Position the other back rods, fanning them out, and fix with roofing nails.

8 Make the decorative apron. Skim the ends of the components to a flat-faced finish; nail to the rails with roofing nails. Fix the diagonal long rail to the legs with clenched 125–150 mm nails.

DESIGN VARIATIONS

1

2

3

(1) Classic Victorian three-seater design with additional legs at the centre.
(2) A design inspired by Chinese motifs, perfect for an oriental-style garden. (3) English Gothic design with pointed arch imagery.

LIVING WILLOW ARCH

B*uilding the living willow arch is a really magical procedure. It starts with a rather flimsy structure made from posts and rods, which is soon transformed into a beautiful, living hedge. It is a wonderfully easy project. We built the framework in late winter, pushed the willow hedgerow cuttings into the ground in early spring, and then we simply watched and waited. The photograph shows the arch after one year's growth.*

YOU WILL NEED

Materials for an arch approximately 2.15 m high and 900 mm wide, with 2 m of fence either side.

- Larch poles with the bark removed and one end cut to a point: 8 poles, 2 m long and 60–70 mm in diameter (uprights)

- Beech coppice: 4 rods, 4 m long and 15–20 mm in diameter (arch)

- Beech coppice: 8 rods, 3 m long and 15–20 mm in diameter (woven horizontal rails)

- Willow: 36 cuttings, about 180 mm long

- Galvanized nails: 1 kg pack of 75 mm x 3.75 mm

- Galvanized wire: small roll of soft 1 mm wire

Tools

- Pencil and flexible rule

- Sledgehammer

- Long-nosed pliers

- Stepladder

- Claw hammer

- Long-handled loppers or secateurs

PERSPECTIVE VIEW OF THE ARCH

Arch
15–20 mm beech rod, cut to fit

Woven horizontal rail
15–20 mm beech rod, cut to fit

Uprights are spaced 700–900 mm apart

Uprights are spaced 900 mm apart

Willow cuttings
Obtain cuttings that are about 180 mm long, and space them 100 mm apart

Upright
60–70 mm larch pole, 2 m long (300 mm in ground)

HOW TO MAKE THE LIVING WILLOW ARCH

1 Measure out the position of the eight uprights. The archway is 900 mm wide, while the other uprights can be set about 700–900 mm apart. Using the sledgehammer, knock the larch poles into the ground to a depth of 300 mm, so that the tops are level (assess this by eye).

2 To make the arch, hold two of the 4 m rods, thin end uppermost, on the inside face of the two uprights for the arch, and wire them in place. Flex the rods repeatedly until they are supple and flexible, then bring them together at top centre, making a rounded arch. Bind the overlaps with at least three straps of wire.

3 Nail the thick ends of the other two 4 m rods to the tops of the three outermost uprights on each side. Run the thin ends of the rods in a smooth curve up and over the arch, flexing them and easing in place. Bind with wire.

4 Weave the eight 3 m beech rods in and out of the uprights to make two horizontal rails at either side of the arch. Nail the rods in place and trim the ends with the loppers, so they are flush with the uprights.

5 Trim off the bottom of each willow cutting, to help it establish, and push them into the ground at 100 mm intervals. As the cuttings grow, weave the new growth in and out of the other cuttings and the framework of the arch.

DESIGN VARIATIONS

1

2

3

(1) Linked arches of living willow form an impressive tunnel or curving pergola. (2) An arched framework makes a cosy bower or arbour (combined with a green wood bench). *(3) A living willow wigwam shelter for children to play in.*

HEARTS AND DIAMONDS SCREEN

This screen is both functional and decorative. The bottom section is strong enough to hold back pets and children, and the top is high enough to provide shade, give an element of privacy, and support climbing plants. The primary design detail – the heart set within the frame – is very attractive. Another way of using the design is to build several screens and set them side by side to make a fence.

YOU WILL NEED

Materials *for a screen approximately 1.88 m high and 1.36 m wide.*

- Larch poles: 6 de-barked poles, 2 m long and 60 mm in diameter (main frame)

- Beech coppice: 80 rods, 2 m long and 10–20 mm in diameter (woven lower section, heart shape and diamond lattice)

- Galvanized nails: 1 kg pack of 75 mm x 3.75 mm

- Steel nails: 1 kg pack of 125 mm x 5.6 mm

- Galvanized wire: small roll of soft 1 mm wire

Tools

- Pencil and flexible rule

- Two portable workbenches

- General-purpose, coarse-toothed saw

- Mallet

- Bevel-edged chisel, 40–50 mm wide

- Claw hammer

- Long-nosed pliers

- Long-handled loppers or hand secateurs

PERSPECTIVE VIEW
OF THE SCREEN

Heart
10–20 mm beech rods, cut to fit

Main frame vertical
60 mm larch pole, 1.88 m long

Diamond lattice
10–20 mm beech rods, cut to fit

Woven lower section
10–20 mm beech rods, cut to fit

Main frame horizontal
60 mm larch pole, 1.36 m long

HOW TO MAKE THE HEARTS AND DIAMONDS SCREEN

1 Cut the six larch poles for the main frame to length: three verticals at 1.88 m long and three horizontals at 1.36 m. To make the lap joints, measure 160 mm along from the ends of all the poles and saw halfway through the 60 mm diameter. Run the saw cut so that it angles towards the end of the pole.

2 Once you have sawn halfway through the diameter, take the mallet and chisel and chop directly into the end of the pole, so that the split travels into the saw cut and the waste falls away. For the central laps, make two angled saw cuts and clear the waste wood by slicing, at a low angle, into the cuts.

3 Lay the three vertical poles parallel on the grass, with the cut-away sections uppermost. Place the horizontal poles in position so that all the joints are nicely mated, and then hammer one 125 mm nail through each intersection. Turn the frame over and bang the points of the nails over and back down into the wood to clench the joints tight.

4 Take about 50 of the thickest beech rods and weave them alternately in and out of the three vertical poles, to make up the panel at the bottom of the frame. Select the wood carefully so that neighbouring rods fit together snugly. Use the mallet to pack the rods tight and to bang the ends level. Nail the ends with 75 mm nails.

5 Nail beech rods diagonally across the top of the frame with 75 mm nails, to form one side of the lattice. Turn it over so that the lattice is on the underside. Bind three of the thinner beech rods together with wire, then ease them into the top of the frame to form a portion of the heart shape. Wire it to the main frame. Repeat this procedure to finish the heart motif.

6 Nail another set of rods in place with 75 mm nails, so that they cross the first set, and so that the bundles of rods making up the heart are contained. If necessary, use additional wire binding to hold the bundles in place. Trim the ends of all the rods to a tidy finish with the loppers or secateurs. Stand the screen in position and push the verticals into the ground.

DESIGN VARIATIONS

1   2   3

(1) A traditional design incorporating diamond motifs at the top. (2) A design that negates the need to weave the rods – the pattern is formed by nailed rods. (3) A classic design that uses a Roman arch motif at the top of the screen.

RUSTIC PAVILION PERGOLA

O ne of the swiftest ways of creating a large design statement in a garden is to build a pergola. Pergolas are versatile – depending on its size and strength, a pergola can be a frame for your grapevines, the central feature of your rose garden, a place for a swing, a pavilion over your barbecue area, or whatever else inspires you.

YOU WILL NEED

Materials for a pergola approximately 2.1 m high, 2 m wide and 3.7 m long.

- Marking sticks: 6 short sticks

- Larch posts: 6 posts, 3 m long and 100 mm in diameter (vertical posts)

- Larch posts: 8 posts, 2 m long and 100 mm in diameter (main beams, banister rails, footrails)

- Larch posts: 7 posts, 2 m long and 80 mm in diameter (rafters)

- Beech mature coppice: 3 poles, 3 m long and 50 mm in diameter (diagonal braces)

- Hazel coppice: 11 rods, 3 m long and 20–25 mm in diameter (decorative balustrade)

- Steel nails: 1 kg pack of 150 mm x 6 mm, 1 kg pack of 100 mm x 4.5 mm

- Hardcore: 6 buckets of builder's rubble

- Temporary braces: 2 poles, about 2 m long (for setting up the pergola)

Tools

- Pencil and flexible rule
- Ball of twine
- Club hammer
- Spade
- Sledgehammer
- Stepladder

- Measuring board, 2 m long

- General-purpose, coarse-toothed saw

- Spirit level

- Two portable workbenches

- Small axe

- Cordless drill

- Drill bits to fit the size of your nails

- Claw hammer

- Long-handled loppers or secateurs

PERSPECTIVE VIEW OF THE PERGOLA

Main beam
100 mm larch post, 3.7 m long

Banister rail
100 mm larch post, 1.44 m long

Decorative balustrade
20–25 mm hazel rods, cut to fit

Hardcore

Rafter
80 mm larch post, 2 m long

Vertical post
100 mm larch post, 3 m long

Diagonal brace
50 mm beech pole, cut to fit

Footrail
100 mm larch post, 1.44 m long

HOW TO MAKE THE RUSTIC PAVILION PERGOLA

1 Use the rule, twine, club hammer and marking sticks to establish the position of the six vertical posts. Set the three front posts 1.5 m apart, the three back posts likewise, with the aisle between them measuring 1.3 m. Check that the diagonal measurements are identical.

2 Dig a hole, 300 mm deep, for each vertical post. Fill the hole with 100 mm of hardcore, stand the post on it and prop it up with the temporary braces. Pack more hardcore into the hole, compacting it with the sledgehammer and club hammer. Set all six vertical posts in place.

3 Use the measuring board to establish a point 2 m above ground level on one vertical post. Saw through the post at this point. Cut the tops of the other five posts level with this.

4 Cut a 100 mm-long half-lap on one end of each main beam. (Mark 100 mm from the end, saw halfway through the post's diameter, and remove the waste with the axe.)

5 Position the main beams on top of the vertical posts, centring the lap joints on the middle posts. Spike in place with 150 mm nails (drill pilot holes to avoid splitting the wood).

6 Position the rafters on top of the beams, directly above the central vertical posts, and fix with 150 mm nails. Make sure that all the rafters are square to the main beams and parallel.

7 Using a saw, hammer and 150 mm nails, fix the banister and footrails to the three front vertical posts. (Footrails 100 mm above ground level; banisters 800 mm above ground level.)

8 Make the diagonal braces: the 600 mm-long braces between the vertical posts, main beams and rafters, and the two that link the three back vertical posts. Fix with 100 mm nails.

9 Use the eleven hazel coppice rods to make the decorative balustrading – the two curved bows, and the rods that fan out from the centre of the two footrails. Use 100 mm nails to fix the rods in place. Finally, use the loppers and saw to trim all the wood to a neat finish.

DESIGN VARIATIONS

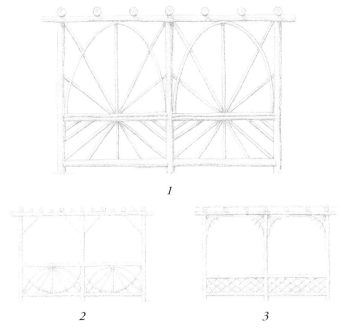

1

2   *3*

(1) A classic arched design with a sunburst pattern. (2) A design featuring double curves under the banister. (3) An American folk art design with "gingerbread" brackets and a diamond pattern border.

COUNTRY CLUB CHAIR

*T*his *beautifully curvaceous chair draws its inspiration from the generously large porch and loggia armchairs our family used to have back in the late 1950s. This chair is surprisingly easy to build. All you do is set up the four-square frame, and then bend the wands around and down to make the arms and back.*

YOU WILL NEED

Materials for a chair approximately 845 mm high, 700 mm wide and 865 mm deep.

☞ Beech mature coppice: 6 poles, 3 m long and 40–50 mm in diameter (legs, rails and diagonal stretchers)

☞ Beech coppice: 1 rod, 3 m long and 15–20 mm in diameter (rail bracers)

☞ Beech coppice: 10 rods, 2 m long and 25–30 mm in diameter (seat, back and seat trimmers)

☞ Beech coppice: 20 wands, 3 m long and 10–15 mm in diameter (arms, backrest and decorative underarm detail)

☞ Galvanized cap-end roofing nails: 1 kg pack of 75 mm

☞ Galvanized nails: 1 kg pack of 100 mm x 4.5 mm, 1 kg pack of 75 mm x 3.75 mm, 1 kg pack of 40 mm x 2.65 mm

Tools

☞ Pencil, flexible rule and square

☞ Portable workbench

☞ General-purpose, coarse-toothed saw

☞ Small axe

☞ Chopping log

☞ Plywood workboard about 1.5 m square

☞ Cordless drill

☞ Twist bits to fit the various nail sizes

☞ Claw hammer

☞ Long-handled loppers

☞ Hand secateurs

PERSPECTIVE VIEW OF THE CHAIR

Underarm detail
Two 10–15 mm wands, cut to fit

Backrest
10–15 mm wand, cut to fit

Seat
25–30 mm rod, 650 mm long

Front leg
40–50 mm pole, 500 mm long

Seat trimmer
25–30 mm rod, 445 mm long

Front rail
40–50 mm pole, 650 mm long

Back
25–30 mm rod, 650 mm long

Back leg
40–50 mm pole, 777 mm long

Side rail
40–50 mm pole, 650 mm long

Diagonal stretcher
40–50 mm pole, cut to fit

Rail bracer
15–20 mm rod, cut to fit

HOW TO MAKE THE COUNTRY CLUB CHAIR

1 Saw all the straight members for the chair to length – everything except the wood that is to be bent (the beech coppice wands that make the backrest). Use the axe to skim flat faces on the ends of the rails and rail bracers, and the rods that make the seat.

2 Set two legs, two rails and two rail bracers flat on the workboard, so that they make one side of the chair. The legs should be 460 mm apart on the inside edges. Make checks with the square, drill pilot holes through the topmost rods, and fix with 100 mm nails.

3 Make the other side. Each side of the chair is a mirror image copy of the other. Link them up with the rails and rail bracers. The chair sides should be 445 mm apart on the inside edges.

4 Cut the diagonal stretchers to a very tight push-fit and nail them in place with 75 mm nails, with the nails running from the ends of the stretchers and into the legs.

5 Make the seat. Arrange the seat rods from front to back of the chair. Fix to the top of the rails. Nail a trimmer piece to cover the front ends of the rods. Use roofing nails throughout.

6 Nail a second trimmer across the seat rods, so that it butts hard up against the two back legs. One at a time, bend and nail the backrest wands to the top of the legs with 40 mm nails.

7 Position the seat back rods, nailing the bottom ends to the trimmer. Fan out the rods and nail the top ends through the curved wands. Use 75 mm nails throughout.

8 Fix the underarm detail wands (inside the front legs, under the arms, round the back to the back rails). Fix eight wands to make the back and arm shape. Use 40 mm nails throughout.

DESIGN VARIATIONS

1

2

3

(1) Traditional American folk art design with "twisted ribbon" arms.
(2) Bow-backed design with naturally bent rustic legs and an extra-wide seat. (3) High-backed design complemented by "ribbon" arms.

CANTILEVER BRIDGE

If you want to create a really big, impressive project, you can't do much better than this bridge, which is great fun to build. If the idea of living the life of a pioneer, building log cabins and suspension bridges over river canyons appeals to you, this project will give you a taste of what it was like to be an early American settler.

YOU WILL NEED

Materials for a bridge approximately 1.8 m high, 1.3 m wide and 3.7 m long.

- Larch: 2 straight young trees, 4 m long and 130 mm in diameter (two main beams)

- Larch: 2 posts, 2 m long and 130 mm in diameter (four piles)

- Larch: 5 posts, 3 m long and 100 mm in diameter (walkway surface)

- Larch: 3 posts, 2 m long and 100 mm in diameter (walkway cantilevers)

- Beech mature coppice: 4 bow-shaped poles, 4 m long and 40–50 mm in diameter (banister rails)

- Beech mature coppice: 6 poles, 3 m long and 40–50 mm in diameter (rail supports)

- Beech mature coppice: 4 poles, 2 m long and 40–50 mm in diameter (rail support braces)

- Steel nails: 2 kg pack of 125 mm x 5.6 mm, 2 kg pack of 150 mm x 6 mm

Tools

- Pencil and flexible rule

- Portable workbench

- General-purpose, coarse-toothed saw

- Small axe

- Chopping log

- Sledgehammer

- Cordless drill

- Twist bits to fit the various nail sizes

- Mallet

- Claw hammer

PERSPECTIVE VIEW
OF THE BRIDGE

Banister rail
40–50 mm bow-shaped beech pole, 3.35 m long

Walkway cantilever
100 mm split larch post, 1.3 m long

Rail support
40–50 mm beech pole, 1 m long

Rail support brace
40–50 mm beech pole, cut to fit

Walkway surface
100 mm split larch post, 600 mm long

Main beam
130 mm larch post, 3.7 m long

Pile
130 mm larch post, 600 mm long

HOW TO MAKE THE CANTILEVER BRIDGE

1 Saw the four piles to length at 600 mm long, and use the axe to shape the ends into a point. Pair the piles 140 mm apart – positioning them at either side of the pond – and bang them into the ground with the sledgehammer, so that the top ends are level with each other. Drill and nail the two main beams in place with 150 mm nails.

2 Cut the walkway surface posts and cantilevers to length; use the axe and mallet to split them in half. Position the cantilevers four logs in at each end, and one in the centre. Axe away part of the ends of three walkway pieces to accommodate the rail supports. Nail the walkway surface posts and cantilevers across the two main beams (use 125 mm nails).

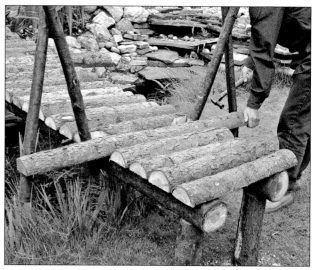

3 Cut the twelve rail supports to length at 1 m long, and arrange them in well-matched pairs. Take one pair of supports at a time and drill, nail and clench them at a point about 200 mm along from the end, so as to make an "X" shape. Use 150 mm nails.

4 Set the crossed rail supports in position, so that they are at the correct height (top end about 655 mm above the walkway surface), balanced, and with the intersection at the top. Drill and nail them to the extended ends of the walkway cantilevers, using 150 mm nails.

5 Set the top banister rails in place so that they are cupped by the top of the crossed rail supports, and fix them with clenched 150 mm nails. You will need help to bend and ease the rails into place. Fix the lower banister rails on the underside of the crossed rail supports with 125 mm nails.

6 Cut the eight rail support braces to length and nail the bottom ends to the bottom of the crossed rail supports, and the top ends to the middle of the lower banister rails. Use 125 mm nails. To give the structure extra strength, clench over the nails on the outside of the rails.

DESIGN VARIATIONS

1

2

3

(1) A design including steps leading down a sloping bank to a bridge. (2) Traditional design with curved handrail and twisted rail details. (3) This design draws its inspiration from the images on Chinese willow pattern china.

"TEA FOR TWO" SHELTER

P*icture yourself and a companion whiling away a warm summer's afternoon in this shaded shelter, with a pot of tea for two. What could be more delightful? The shelter also provides a place to enjoy the garden throughout the seasons.*

YOU WILL NEED

Materials for a shelter approximately 3.5 m high and 1.7 m in diameter.

- Larch : 16 posts, 3 m long and 140 mm in diameter (six vertical posts, horizontal rails and roof finial)

- Larch: 3 posts, 2 m long and 100 mm in diameter (floor joists)

- Larch: 6 twisted character poles, 2 m long and 40–60 mm in diameter (decorative banister rails)

- Beech mature coppice: 3 poles, 2 m long and 60 mm in diameter (roof rafters)

- Beech mature coppice: 8 poles, 2 m long and 40 mm in diameter (roof ties, diagonal wall braces and wall brackets)

- Hazel coppice: 9 rods, 2 m long and 20–25 mm in diameter (roof and wall trim, straight banister rails)

- Sawn boards: 10 treated boards, 2 m long, 150 mm wide and 20 mm thick (floorboards and sills)

- Feather-edge cladding (rough-sawn): 180 x 2 m long, 100 mm wide and 10 mm thick (three back walls and roof, felt supports)

- Steel nails: 3 kg pack of 150 mm x 6 mm, 2 kg pack of 125 mm x 5.6 mm, 2 kg pack of 100 mm x 4.5 mm

- Galvanized nails: 2 kg pack of 40 mm x 2.65 mm

- Concrete blocks/slabs: 6 or more (post pads)

- Plastic sheeting: a piece of medium-grade plastic sheeting, about 3 m square

- Roofing felt: 1 roll of medium-grade roofing felt, 1 m wide and 10 m long

- Flashing: 2 m self-adhesive flashing, 30 mm wide

Tools

- Pencil, felt-tip pen and flexible rule

- Two portable workbenches

- General-purpose, coarse-toothed saw

- Mallet

- Large chisel

- Cordless drill

- Drill bits to fit the size of your nails

- Claw hammer

- Ball of twine

- Spirit level and 2 m length of board

- Stepladder

- Small axe

- Craft knife and a pair of old scissors

- Long-handled loppers or secateurs

- Hand secateurs

PERSPECTIVE VIEW OF THE SHELTER

EXPLODED VIEW OF THE SHELTER

Roof finial
*140 mm larch post,
1 m long*

Optional finial decoration
Pine cones wired to post

Flashing
(to stop rain getting through)

Felt

Roof rafter
*60 mm beech pole,
1.32 m long*

Felt support
*Feather-edge cladding,
cut to fit*

Roof tie
*40 mm beech pole,
cut to fit*

Roof trim
*20–25 mm hazel rods,
cut to fit*

Roof cladding
*Feather-edge board,
100 mm x 10 mm,
cut to fit*

Diagonal wall bracket
*40 mm beech pole,
cut to fit*

Wall cladding
*Feather-edge board,
100 mm x 10 mm,
cut to fit*

Diagonal wall brace
*40 mm beech pole,
cut to fit*

Sill
*150 mm x 20 mm board
cut to fit*

Wall trim
*20–25 mm hazel rod,
cut to fit*

**Decorative
banister rail**
*40–60 mm larch
character pole,
1.08 m long*

Vertical post
*140 mm larch post,
2.2 m long*

Straight banister rail
*20–25 mm hazel rod,
1.08 m long*

Floor joist
*100 mm larch post,
cut to fit*

Floorboard
*150 mm x 20 mm board.
Lengths cut to fit*

Horizontal rail
*140 mm larch post,
750 mm long*

HOW TO MAKE THE "TEA FOR TWO" SHELTER

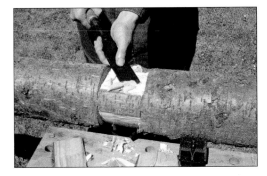

1 Cut the six vertical posts. Use the diagram to mark the position of the rails at roof, banister and floor level. Cut out the housings (at an angle of 60°) for the ends of the horizontal rails.

2 Pair the vertical posts on the grass. Nail the nine horizontal rails (ends angled back at 60°) in place. Fix the wall brackets across the top corners. Use 150 mm nails throughout.

3 Level the site and cover with plastic sheet. Draw a circle with a radius of 850 mm. Lay a concrete block for each vertical post (make sure they are at more or less the same level).

4 Set the paired vertical posts on the concrete blocks (make sure the entrance is facing in the correct direction) and use temporary props to hold them in place. Link the posts with the remaining horizontal rails. Use the spirit level to ensure that the posts are upright.

5 Set the the two outer floor joists in place, supported on offcuts and nailed to the posts, also the middle joist (housed at front and back, and nailed to the rails). Use 150 mm nails. Note how the middle housing is lapped to take the downward thrust of the weight of the floor.

6 Nail the floorboards across the joists with 100 mm nails. Work from the front of the shelter to the back, so that the doorstep is made from a single complete board width.

7 Set three of the most bowed roof tie poles across the walls, so that they go over and under each other to link opposite vertical posts. Nail to the top of the posts with 100 mm nails.

8 Cut the roof finial to length and use the saw, mallet and chisel to cut a ring housing for the end of the rafters. Sculpt the top of the post to a decorative point with the axe.

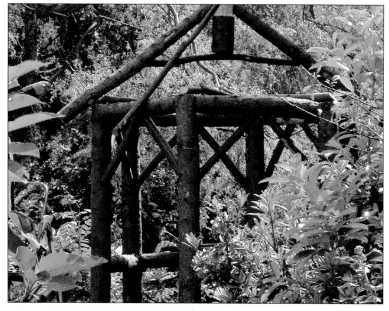

9 Build a roof A-frame with the finial post, two of the rafters and a length of beech offcut. Position the frame to span the walls, propping it upright with a temporary stay. Nail the A-frame to the top of the vertical posts and then fix the other four rafters in place. Use 125 mm nails.

10 Nail lengths of feather-edge cladding across the roof, to support the roofing felt. With craft knife and scissors, cut the roofing felt to size. One triangle at a time, and starting at the bottom, cover the roof with sheets of overlapping felt. Cut and fix the cladding, flashing and pine cones.

11 Starting just above ground level, cut the cladding to length and drill and nail it in place across the outside of the three back bays or panels, using 40 mm nails. Position the cladding so that the waney edge is displayed. Do your best to centre the ends of the cladding, or the sides of neighbouring panels, so that they meet in a straight line on the posts.

12 Finally, when you have cut and fitted the two sills, the various diagonal wall braces and the roof trim that covers the ends of the cladded roof and wall panels, use the twisted character poles and hazel rods to make the decorative banister rails and straight banister rails. Nail in position with 100 mm nails. Tidy up ends with the loppers and secateurs.

DESIGN VARIATIONS

1   *2*   *3*

(1) *A design featuring a low roof, suitable for exposed windy sites.* **(2)** *An open-sided design, intended to encourage* climbing plants to cover the sides. **(3)** *A rectangular shelter or arbour with lattice sides and a lovers' seat inside.*

SUPPLIERS

All types of green wood, from large sections to small sections, should be purchased from managed woodlands in your area. Consult the telephone directory for details of local wood suppliers. Other materials such as nails, wire and twine, and all the tools featured in this book, are available from general DIY stores.

UK

Green wood information

Forestry Commission H.Q.
231 Crostophine Road
Edinburgh
Scotland EH12 7AT
Tel: (0131) 334 0303

General DIY Outlets (branches nationwide)

B & Q plc
Head Office:
Portswood House
1 Hampshire Corporate Park
Chandlers Ford
Eastleigh
Hants SO53 3YX
Tel: (01703) 256256
(Branches nationwide)

Focus Do-It-All Group Ltd
Head Office:
Gawsworth House
Westmere Drive
Crewe
Cheshire CW1 6XB
Tel: (01384) 456456
(Branches nationwide)

Homebase Ltd
Beddington House
Railway Approach
Wallington
Surrey SM6 0HB
Tel: (020) 8784 7200
(Branches nationwide)

AUSTRALIA

DIY stores

Mitre 10
319 George Street
Sydney NSW 2000
Tel: (02) 9262 1435
(Outlets nationwide)

BBC Hardware & Hardwarehouse
Head Office, Bldg A
Cnr. Cambridge & Chester Streets
Epping NSW 2121
Tel: (02) 9876 0888
(Outlets nationwide)

NEW ZEALAND

DIY stores

Mitre 10
Head Office:
182 Wairau Rd
Glenfield, Auckland
Tel: (09) 443 9900
(Outlets nationwide)

Placemakers Support Office
150 Marua Rd
Private Bag 14942,
Panmure
Auckland
Tel: (09) 525 5100

INDEX